AUG 1 0 2020

W9-DAN-733

FREEDOM'S PROMISE

DENNIS BANKS AND RUSSELL MEANS
NATIVE AMERICAN ACTIVISTS

BY DUCHESS HARRIS, JD, PHD
WITH A. R. CARSER

Core Library

Cover image: Activists Russell Means, *left*, and Dennis Banks, *right*, raised awareness of Native civil rights issues.

An Imprint of Abdo Publishing
abdobooks.com

abdobooks.com

Published by Abdo Publishing, a division of ABDO, PO Box 398166, Minneapolis, Minnesota 55439. Copyright © 2020 by Abdo Consulting Group, Inc. International copyrights reserved in all countries. No part of this book may be reproduced in any form without written permission from the publisher. Core Library™ is a trademark and logo of Abdo Publishing.

Printed in the United States of America, North Mankato, Minnesota
092019
012020

THIS BOOK CONTAINS
RECYCLED MATERIALS

Cover Photo: Bettmann/Getty Images
Interior Photos: Bettmann/Getty Images, 1, 34–35; Michelle Vignes/Gamma-Rapho/Getty Images, 5, 12–13, 43; Paul Slade/Paris Match/Getty Images, 6–7; Everett Collection/Newscom, 9, 15; Red Line Editorial, 11, 30; AP Images, 20–21, 32; Darryl Dyck/The Canadian Press/AP Images, 26–27; Library of Congress, 29; Eric Risberg/AP Images, 39; Ed Andrieski/AP Images, 40

Editor: Maddie Spalding
Series Designer: Ryan Gale

Library of Congress Control Number: 2019941999

Publisher's Cataloging-in-Publication Data

Names: Harris, Duchess, author. | Carser, A. R., author.
Title: Dennis Banks and Russell Means: Native American activists / by Duchess Harris and A. R. Carser
Other title: Native American activists
Description: Minneapolis, Minnesota : Abdo Publishing, 2020 | Series: Freedom's promise | Includes online resources and index.
Identifiers: ISBN 9781532190810 (lib. bdg.) | ISBN 9781532176661 (ebook)
Subjects: LCSH: Banks, Dennis (Nowa Cumig)--Juvenile literature. | Means, Russell, 1939-2012--Juvenile literature. | American Indian Movement--Juvenile literature. | Red Power movement--Juvenile literature. | Indigenous peoples--Civil rights--Biography--Juvenile literature. | Native Americans--Biography--Juvenile literature.
Classification: DDC 973.049700--dc23

CONTENTS

A LETTER FROM DUCHESS

I grew up in the 1970s. In our home, we talked about Black activists and their fight for civil rights. At the same time, Native Americans were also fighting for their rights. The American Indian Movement (AIM) was very active. AIM was a civil rights group that protested the US government's mistreatment of Native Americans. For centuries, US officials had been pushing Native Americans off their lands. Native Americans still struggled for control of their lands in the 1970s. AIM leaders Dennis Banks and Russell Means were at the forefront of this fight to regain civil rights.

I am so pleased to write a book that centralizes the work of Banks and Means. These men grew up in different communities, but they had similar goals. They led civil rights protests and helped AIM gain international recognition.

I hope you enjoy learning about these influential activists. Please join me on a journey that explores the history of AIM and the legacies of Banks and Means.

Russell Means, *left*, **and Dennis Banks,** *right*, **were key leaders of the**
American Indian Movement (AIM).

CHAPTER
ONE

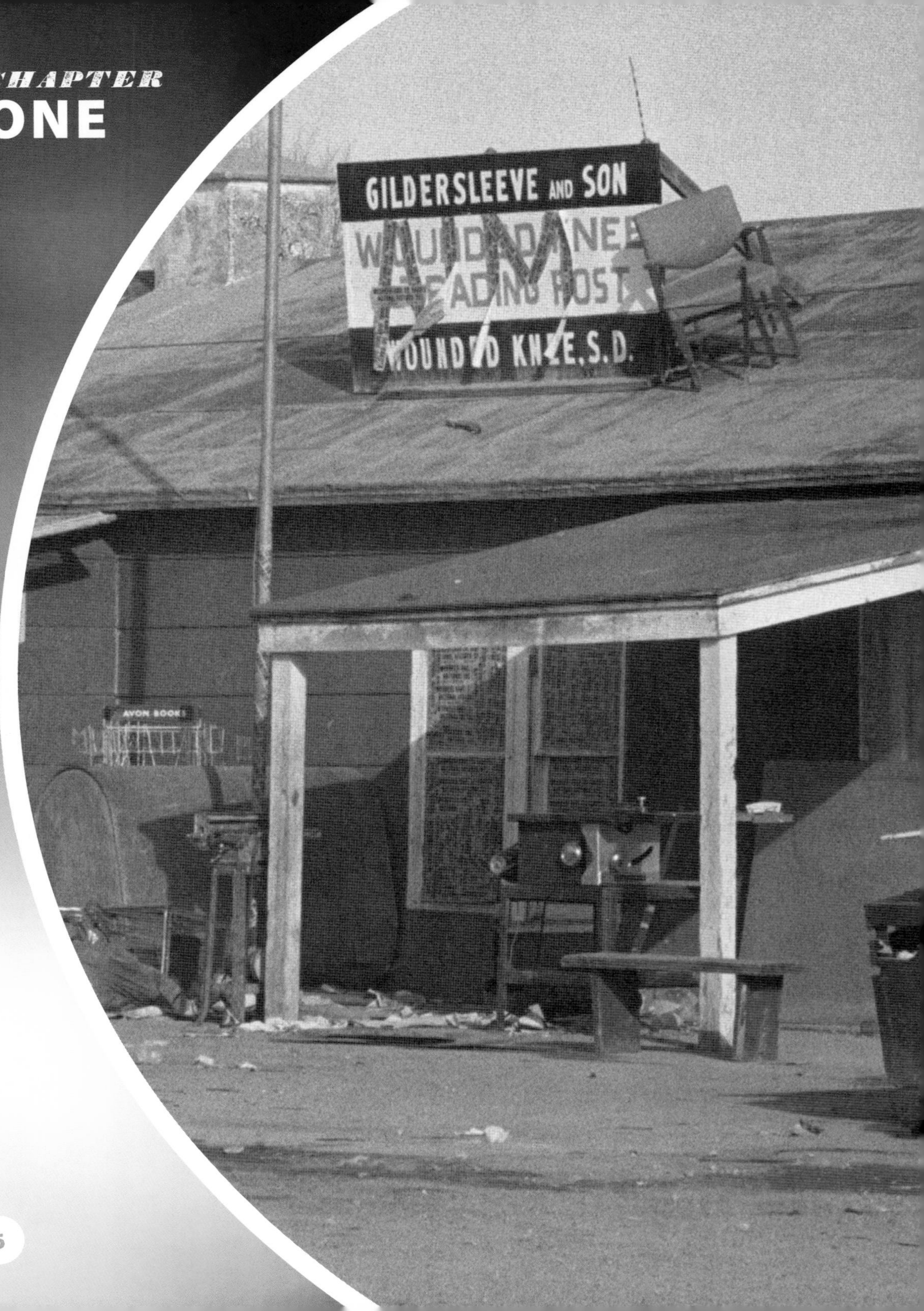

OCCUPYING WOUNDED KNEE

The plains of Wounded Knee in South Dakota were dark and cold on February 27, 1973. The windows of the houses were blacked out. Activists and members of the Oglala Lakota community waited inside the houses. Suddenly, gunshots blasted in the distance. A military aircraft flew overhead. Military vehicles circled the community.

A few hours earlier, approximately 250 activists had traveled to Wounded Knee. Wounded Knee was a town on the Pine Ridge Reservation. Members of

Native American activists occupied many buildings, including a trading post, in the Wounded Knee occupation of 1973.

the Oglala Lakota Nation lived on this reservation. Some residents were unhappy with the reservation's leadership. Community elders had asked the activists to help them remove the current leadership.

The activists were part of the American Indian Movement (AIM). AIM advocated for the rights of Native Americans. Dennis Banks and Russell Means were among the AIM activists at Wounded Knee. The activists had decided to occupy the town. An occupation is a type of protest. It involves taking control of an area until certain demands are met.

Banks speaks to other Native activists at the occupation of Wounded Knee.

One of the group's demands was a change to tribal leadership. Another was a demand directed at the US government. AIM wanted to review all the treaties the government had with Native nations. It wanted Native people to have more control over their living situations and their lands. This idea is known as self-determination.

CENTURIES OF CONFLICT

Activists were aware of Wounded Knee's significance. The town is an important place for the Lakota and other Native peoples. In 1890 US soldiers ambushed Lakota elders, women, and children camped along Wounded Knee Creek. The soldiers murdered more than 200 Lakota people.

The Wounded Knee massacre is part of a long history of violence against Native people. In 1973 many people were frustrated by the government's continued mistreatment of Native Americans. AIM activists hoped an occupation of Wounded Knee would bring national attention to this issue.

Federal Bureau of Investigation (FBI) agents surrounded Wounded Knee on the night of February 27. The siege went on for 71 days. Agents cut off the town's electricity and water. They tried to stop supplies of food and water from being passed to the activists.

THE PINE RIDGE RESERVATION

Today, the Pine Ridge Reservation is home to approximately 20,000 members of the Oglala Lakota Nation. The Oglala Sioux Tribal Council governs the reservation. There are few jobs available on or near the reservation. Many families are very poor. The tribal council provides some services and jobs. The school district provides jobs and education for people who live on the reservation. Schools teach students the Lakota language and culture.

GOVERNMENT ACTIONS

POLICY OR ACTION	RESULTS	NATIVE NATIONS AFFECTED
Indian Wars, 1768–1889	These wars displaced Native peoples from their lands.	Native nations across the present-day United States
Indian Removal Act, 1830	This act forced Native peoples east of the Mississippi River to move to Indian Territory in present-day Oklahoma.	More than 60 tribes and nations in the present-day United States
The Trail of Tears, 1830s	US soldiers forced Native Americans to march to Oklahoma, resulting in the deaths of thousands of people.	Southeastern nations, including the Cherokee, Creek, Chickasaw, Choctaw, and Seminole
Wounded Knee Massacre, 1890	US troops murdered more than 200 Lakota people.	The Oglala Lakota Nation

This chart shows some of the US government's policies and actions against Native Americans. How do you think the legacy of these policies and actions continues to affect Native communities today?

There were moments of violent conflict during the siege. By May, FBI agents had killed two activists. But on May 8, agents and activists reached an agreement. The siege ended. Banks and Means turned themselves in. They were charged with 11 different crimes, including assault. They would stand trial in 1974. But they were not intimidated. They had both confronted the US government before. They were prepared to fight for the rights of Native people.

BECOMING DENNIS BANKS

Dennis Banks was born on April 12, 1937, on the Leech Lake Reservation. This reservation is in north-central Minnesota. Dennis was a member of the Leech Lake Band of Ojibwe. He was called Nowa-Cumig, which means "at the center of the universe." The land his family lived on holds special meaning for the Ojibwe people. They believe it is the place where the Creator made the Western Hemisphere.

BOARDING SCHOOL

Dennis spent his early childhood on the Leech Lake Reservation. He lived with six

As a leader of AIM, Banks, *middle*, encouraged Native Americans to come together to stand up for their civil rights.

family members, including his two siblings and his grandparents. He was taken away from his family when he was just five years old. The BIA required Leech Lake families to send their children to boarding school. These schools were often hundreds of miles away from the children's homes.

By the early 1900s, the US government had built many Native boarding schools throughout the country. The schools taught all classes in English. Teachers wanted students to forget their Native languages. They also taught Anglo-American culture and traditions. These were the cultures and traditions of white Americans. Each student's hair was cut short. All students were forced to wear gray uniforms.

Dennis was forced to attend Pipestone Indian School in Pipestone, Minnesota. After nine years, he had forgotten most of his native Anishinaabe language. His teachers taught him to hate his Native identity.

At Native boarding schools such as Carlisle Indian Industrial School in Pennsylvania, students had to follow a strict dress code.

In 1953 Dennis ran away from boarding school. He was 16 years old. He traveled more than 280 miles (450 km) north to Bemidji, Minnesota. He rode freight trains to get there. He also walked and hitchhiked. From Bemidji, he traveled east to rejoin his family on the Leech Lake Reservation.

CIVIL RIGHTS

In 1954 Banks joined the US Air Force. He was stationed in Japan. He saw a peaceful civil rights protest while there. Thousands of Buddhist monks and nuns sat in the streets. They were protesting the US military's actions. Japanese officials responded to the protest with violence. Police officers beat the protesters with sticks. This experience left a strong impression on Banks.

After leaving the air force, Banks moved to Minneapolis, Minnesota. In 1966 Banks and a friend stole groceries to feed their families. Banks had a wife and eight children at the time. The police arrested Banks and his friend.

Banks served two years in prison for theft. The prison library had books about Native history and the American civil rights movement. The civil rights movement was a period of mass protests. The protests helped African Americans gain equal rights. The movement gained momentum in the 1950s and 1960s.

Banks read all the books he could find on these topics. He wanted to create a civil rights movement for Native people.

FOUNDING AIM

Banks was released from prison in 1968. He and his friend George Mitchell had an idea for a Native civil rights organization. Clyde Bellecourt also became part of the group. They called their organization the American Indian Movement (AIM).

Police brutality was the first civil rights issue AIM

PERSPECTIVES
CLYDE BELLECOURT

Clyde Bellecourt was AIM's first chairman. He is an Ojibwe activist. His Ojibwe name is Nee-gon-we-way-we-dun, or "Thunder before the Storm." He attended AIM's first meeting in 1968. He has been working with AIM since then. In 2017 Bellecourt remembered how he and Banks viewed AIM. He said, "We did look at our organization as a civil and human rights organization. . . . Every one of our treaties encompasses civil and human rights. If the government lived up to its treaties, we wouldn't have needed the American Indian Movement."

DISCRIMINATION

In the 1960s, southeast Minneapolis was home to many Native Americans. They did not have many job opportunities. Public schools did not teach children about Native history. Minneapolis police officers targeted Native Americans. They went to bars where Native people hung out. They arrested everyone in the bars. They made up charges for their arrests.

wanted to address. Police often targeted and unfairly arrested Native Americans. AIM created an all-Native patrol that alerted people when police were coming. As police rounded up Native Americans, AIM leaders took photos. They brought these photos to the Minneapolis Police Department to prove that police officers were abusing them.

In 1969 Banks went to a conference in Minneapolis. There, he met a young activist from Cleveland, Ohio. The activist asked Banks to speak at the Cleveland American Indian Center. He also asked how he could become a member of AIM. Banks replied, "You just did!" The young activist was Russell Means.

STRAIGHT TO THE
SOURCE

Banks believed nonviolent protest could help Native Americans gain civil rights. In his autobiography, he wrote:

> As long as American Indians were polite and soft-spoken . . . they got nowhere. African American civil rights had been gained by protests. [AIM chairman] Clyde [Bellecourt] and I decided that in order to get anywhere AIM had to become confrontational—confrontational but not violent. AIM walks with the Canupa, the sacred pipe of peace. If we were to put the pipe away and only carry the gun, our movement would come to nothing.

> Source: Dennis Banks and Richard Erdoes. *Ojibwa Warrior: Dennis Banks and the Rise of the American Indian Movement.* Norman, OK: University of Oklahoma Press, 2004. Print. 105.

Changing Minds

Imagine you are an AIM member who agrees with Banks's opinion on nonviolent protest. How would you explain his perspective to a friend who disagrees with his view? Make sure to explain your opinion. Include facts and details that support your reasons.

BECOMING RUSSELL MEANS

Russell Means was born on November 10, 1939, on the Pine Ridge Reservation. Russell was a member of the Oglala Lakota Nation. As a boy, he was called Wanbli Ohitika, or "Brave Eagle." As a young man, his name was changed in a naming ceremony. He was called Cío, or "Prairie Chicken."

Life on Pine Ridge was difficult. There were few job opportunities. To find steady work, Russell's family traveled between South Dakota and California. In California, they settled near Oakland. In South Dakota, they often lived on or near reservations.

Means organized protests for AIM and was not afraid to stand up against the federal government.

RACISM

Russell first became aware of racism from school. He went to an elementary school in Huron, South Dakota. The school was mostly white. Kids taunted him because he was different from them. Teachers also discriminated against him. One teacher accused him of spreading lice to other kids in the classroom. Lice are small insects that can live on people's bodies. The teacher checked Russell's head in front of the entire class. But she did not find any lice.

Russell did not have to attend boarding school. This was because his family was not living on a reservation at the time. Instead, he attended public schools in California and South Dakota. He was often the only Native person in these schools.

EARLY ACTIVISM

After graduating from high school, Means spent several years trying to hold down steady work in California. Then in 1964, his father invited him to an occupation. The occupation happened on March 9 at Alcatraz Island in San Francisco, California. Activists wanted to reclaim the island for Native peoples. The 1868 Treaty of Fort Laramie said that Native peoples had the right to take back former Native property and lands that the US government no longer used. The federal prison on Alcatraz Island had been closed.

Means and his father represented the Lakota Nation at the occupation. They spent a few hours on the island. Then federal officials forced the occupiers to leave. The US government did not return the island to the Native Americans. But the occupation made the national news. Means had discovered the power of protest.

After the occupation, Means continued to struggle to find long-term employment. He moved to Cleveland for a fresh start in 1968. In April 1969, he opened the Cleveland American Indian Center. It served Native people in the Cleveland area. Programs taught people about their Native cultures and traditions. The center also helped people find jobs and housing.

DISCOVERING AIM

Later in 1969, Means went to San Francisco for a conference. There, he saw Banks and Bellecourt. They were promoting AIM at the conference.

Means and Banks disagree on how they first met. Means says in his autobiography that he received a call from Banks a few weeks after the San Francisco conference. Banks wanted Means to speak at an upcoming conference in Minneapolis. At the conference, Means decided to join AIM. It was the beginning of a long friendship between Means and Banks.

STRAIGHT TO THE
SOURCE

In his autobiography, Means explained how he believed action could spur change. He wrote:

> How does one attain freedom? How can we fight city hall? The BIA? The federal government? How can we succeed in reestablishing our individual rights as guaranteed by the Constitution? It's as simple as this—people of every color must stand up on their hind feet and begin to act like human beings. Start with yourself! Understand that freedom is responsibility. . . . The next step . . . is to organize, organize, organize. Take your message to the streets—but even though government is not going to give away anything, force begets only brutality and injustice. I have swallowed my share of official violence, and I now feel that real change cannot come except through non-violence.

> Source: Russell Means and Marvin J. Wolf. *Where White Men Fear to Tread: The Autobiography of Russell Means*. New York: St. Martin's Press, 1995. Print. 542.

Point of View
Means believed that people are responsible for securing their own freedom. Do you agree? Why or why not?

THE AMERICAN INDIAN MOVEMENT

I n the 1970s, AIM's membership grew. People throughout the United States and in other countries joined the group. AIM was one group within an emerging civil rights movement called the Red Power Movement. Dozens of groups were part of this movement. They worked to help Native Americans regain their rights. They also worked to preserve Native cultures and traditions.

ERASING NATIVE CULTURES

The attempt to erase Native cultures in the United States started more than 200 years

AIM's flag features a peace symbol that also looks like a Native American wearing traditional dress.

WHY *INDIAN*?

In the 1960s, many Native people challenged the term *Indian*. The term can be traced back to Italian explorer Christopher Columbus. He visited some Caribbean islands in the late 1400s. He thought these islands were part of the East Indies. He called the Native people there "Indians." The term *Native American* came into use in the 1960s. But Means and some other Native people preferred the term *American Indian*. In 1968 AIM founders considered dropping *Indian* from their name. But an elder encouraged them to keep it. She said, "Indian is the word they used to oppress us, and Indian is the word we will use to gain our freedom."

before AIM was founded. By the 1800s, the US government had greatly reduced the size of Native-owned territories. The Indian Appropriations Act of 1851 set aside lands for Native nations. These lands were called reservations.

At first, Native nations had control over their reservations. But the 1887 Dawes Act changed that. It divided reservations into portions of land called allotments. The US government

Henry L. Dawes, a senator for Massachusetts, created the Dawes Act.

gave these allotments to individual Native people. This reduced the size of reservations. Native people who accepted allotments became US citizens. As citizens, they were required to follow federal laws. This gave the US government more control over Native peoples' affairs.

In 1934 the Indian Reorganization Act was passed. It ended the allotment system. Then in 1952, the

TIMELINE OF AIM'S ACTIVISM

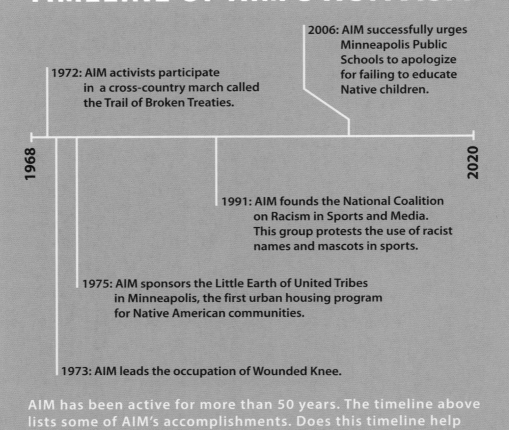

2006: AIM successfully urges Minneapolis Public Schools to apologize for failing to educate Native children.

1972: AIM activists participate in a cross-country march called the Trail of Broken Treaties.

1968

2020

1991: AIM founds the National Coalition on Racism in Sports and Media. This group protests the use of racist names and mascots in sports.

1975: AIM sponsors the Little Earth of United Tribes in Minneapolis, the first urban housing program for Native American communities.

1973: AIM leads the occupation of Wounded Knee.

AIM has been active for more than 50 years. The timeline above lists some of AIM's accomplishments. Does this timeline help you better understand AIM's legacy?

US government adopted a policy called termination.
Its purpose was to eliminate the reservation system.
The government stopped giving tribes and nations
aid and other services. The BIA tried to push many
Native families off reservations and into cities. It set
up job centers in urban areas. It stopped supporting

job programs on reservations. By the 1960s, government policies had effectively destroyed Native self-determination.

THE TRAIL OF BROKEN TREATIES

In the 1970s, AIM activists organized many protests. AIM organized one of its largest marches, called the Trail of Broken Treaties, in 1972. AIM called on activists across West Coast cities to join the march. The activists planned to travel across the country to Washington, DC. They would go to the BIA office in the capital city. Once there, they would present a plan. The plan would allow Native nations to reclaim control of their lands.

AIM'S ACCOMPLISHMENTS

In 1972 AIM opened schools in Minneapolis and Saint Paul, Minnesota. The schools were safe spaces for Native children. Students learned their Native languages. They learned about Native American history and traditions too. AIM activists also worked to improve Native people's living conditions. They distributed food to Native people. They raised money for Native families who lived in poverty.

John Trudell and other AIM activists occupied Alcatraz Island in protest from November 1969 to June 1971.

The activists arrived in Washington, DC, on November 2. The BIA office was closed. Approximately 400 activists entered the building as it opened for the day. Banks and Means were among them.

AIM had arranged meetings with several officials. But no one was there to meet with them. The activists grew frustrated. Some destroyed BIA property. Eventually, AIM leaders spoke with two US senators. The senators promised official hearings on the activists' plan.

On November 9, the activists left Washington, DC. Relations between Native activists and the US government had soured. Three months later, tensions between these groups would result in the clash at Wounded Knee.

EXPLORE ONLINE

Chapter Four talks about how the US government took away Native people's rights and tried to erase their cultures. The website below goes into more depth on this topic. How is the information from the website the same as the information in Chapter Four? What new information did you learn?

RECORDS OF RIGHTS
abdocorelibrary.com/banks-and-means

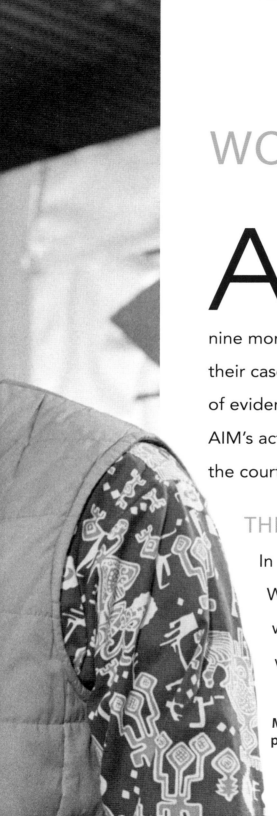

AFTER WOUNDED KNEE

A fter their arrest at Wounded Knee, Banks and Means stood trial in 1974. Their trial lasted more than nine months. In the end, the judge dismissed their cases. The FBI had altered key pieces of evidence. It had also illegally recorded AIM's activities. Some FBI agents had lied to the court.

THE LONGEST WALK

In 1978 AIM leaders organized a walk to Washington, DC. Banks had come up with the idea for this march. The march was a protest against 11 proposed

Means, *left*, and Banks, *right*, spoke to the press in 1974 before their trial.

federal laws. Some of the laws would take away Native people's hunting and fishing rights. One law would cancel all of the government's treaties with Native nations. It would also take away tribal land rights.

The march started in early February in San Francisco. Approximately 2,000 activists participated. Banks and Means were among them. Their 3,000-mile (4,830-km) journey became known as the Longest Walk.

On July 15, the group arrived in Washington, DC. Activists stayed in the capital for more than a week. They arranged rallies and demonstrations. Because of their efforts, none of the 11 bills were passed.

PROTECTING PAHA SAPA

AIM was involved in many other protests throughout the 1970s and 1980s. One protest in 1979 involved a broken treaty. The 1868 Treaty of Fort Laramie promised sacred lands to the Lakota people. The Lakota call these lands Paha Sapa. White Americans call these lands the Black Hills. This mountain range stretches from South

Dakota to Wyoming. The Lakota signed the Treaty of Fort Laramie. But the US government stole the Lakota's lands nine years later. White settlers had found gold in the area. Since then, the Lakota people have fought to reclaim their sacred lands.

In 1979 the US government proposed to allow coal and uranium mining in Paha Sapa. AIM opposed this. The group partnered with ranchers and farmers who lived near the area. Antinuclear activists joined their efforts. These people knew that mining could destroy the land. Together they formed the Black Hills Alliance.

THE LEGAL RIGHTS CENTER

In 1970 AIM activists partnered with African American leaders in Minneapolis. They established the Legal Rights Center (LRC). The LRC provides legal resources for minorities and people living in poverty. Clyde Bellecourt is one of the LRC's founders. Bellecourt and others wanted to provide minorities with good legal protection. Today, police still unjustly arrest Native Americans and other people of color. The LRC helps defend them.

In 1980 the Black Hills Alliance held the Black Hills International Survival Gathering in Piedmont, South Dakota. Approximately 12,000 protesters came. Means spoke at the event. He asked the protesters to help protect Native communities from mining. Today, activists continue to protest mining efforts in Paha Sapa.

PERSPECTIVES

PAHA SAPA

The Lakota and the federal government still fight over the rights to Paha Sapa. The Lakota argue that they have rights to the area. In 1980 the US Supreme Court agreed. Still, the US government did not return the lands to the Lakota. The Supreme Court offered the Lakota $102 million. Today, that amount has grown to more than $1 billion. But the Lakota have never accepted the money. They say their lands were never for sale. Holy Rock was a Lakota tribal president in the early 1960s. He said, "We don't think of the air and water in terms of dollars and cents."

LEGACIES

After the Black Hills protests, Means continued his activism. He traveled to Nicaragua in 1985 and 1986 to support

Banks speaks to students at San Francisco's Alamo Park High School in 1986.

the country's indigenous peoples. The Nicaraguan government was mistreating these people in many ways. It was attacking them and forcing them off their lands.

While Means was in Nicaragua, Banks was serving time in prison. He had been found guilty of rioting and assault in Custer, South Dakota. He had been protesting the release of a white man who had murdered a Native person.

Means, *middle*, participates in a protest march in 1999. The activists marched from the Pine Ridge Reservation to Whiteclay, Nebraska.

Once released from prison, Banks also continued his activism. He organized teach-ins for Native people around the world. Teach-ins are meetings to raise awareness of social or political issues. At Banks's teach-ins, participants learned about other Native tribes and nations.

In 1987 Means ran for US president. He had some support but lost the race. He retired from AIM in 1988.

In the 1990s and 2000s, he appeared in dozens of movies and TV shows.

Banks later moved back to the Leech Lake Reservation. He started a wild rice and maple syrup business in the late 1990s.

Means died at the age of 72 on October 22, 2012. Banks died at the age of 80 on October 29, 2017. People remember them today as powerful activists. They helped improve the lives of Native people. Native activists today continue to build on their legacies.

FURTHER EVIDENCE

Chapter Five explores some of AIM's major protests in the 1970s and 1980s. Identify one of the chapter's main points. What evidence supports this point? Watch the video at the website below. Find a quote from the video that supports this point.

WHAT WAS AIM?
abdocorelibrary.com/banks-and-means

FAST FACTS

- Dennis Banks was an Ojibwe activist. He cofounded the American Indian Movement (AIM) in 1968. AIM is a Native American civil rights group. Banks spent decades fighting for Native people's rights, including the right to self-determination.

- Russell Means was a Lakota activist. He was an active member of AIM. He was an outspoken supporter of Native rights in the United States and around the world.

- AIM helped Native communities in many ways. It opened schools for Native children. It helped Native Americans who were living in poverty. It also organized protests and occupations to raise awareness of Native civil rights issues.

- In 1973 AIM activists occupied Wounded Knee. Banks and Means were among these activists. Wounded Knee is a town on the Pine Ridge Reservation in South Dakota. Activists demanded changes to tribal leadership. They also wanted more control over their lands. US troops laid siege to the town for 71 days. They killed two Native activists. Police later arrested Banks and Means.

- Banks and Means continued to advocate for Native civil rights after the Wounded Knee occupation. Means died in 2012. Banks died in 2017.

STOP AND THINK

Tell the Tale

Chapter Five describes the Longest Walk. Imagine you are a part of this protest. Write 200 words about the journey. What do you see? Why are you participating in this march?

Surprise Me

Chapter Four explores how AIM grew in the 1970s. After reading this book, what two or three facts about AIM did you find most surprising? Write a few sentences about each fact. Why did you find each fact surprising?

Say What?

Studying the Native civil rights movement can mean learning a lot of new vocabulary. Find five words in this book you've never seen before. Use a dictionary to find out what they mean. Then write the meanings in your own words, and use each word in a new sentence.

GLOSSARY

advocate
to publicly support a cause

alliance
a group with shared interests

discrimination
the unjust treatment
of a person or group
based on race or other
perceived differences

indigenous peoples
peoples who originally
settled and lived in an area

poverty
the state of being very poor

racism
the belief that one race is
better than all others

reservation
land in the United
States that is set aside
for Native American
tribes or nations to live on

siege
a military tactic that involves
surrounding people in order
to force them to surrender

treaty
a formal, written agreement
between nations

uranium
a metallic substance mined
for nuclear power

ONLINE
RESOURCES

To learn more about Dennis Banks and Russell Means, visit our free resource websites below.

Visit **abdocorelibrary.com** or scan this QR code for free Common Core resources for teachers and students, including vetted activities, multimedia, and booklinks, for deeper subject comprehension.

Visit **abdobooklinks.com** or scan this QR code for free additional online weblinks for further learning. These links are routinely monitored and updated to provide the most current information available.

LEARN
MORE

Harris, Duchess, JD, PhD, with Kate Conley. *The Indian Removal Act and the Trail of Tears*. Minneapolis, MN: Abdo Publishing, 2020.

Rea, Amy C. *The Trail of Tears*. Minneapolis, MN: Abdo Publishing, 2017.

ABOUT THE
AUTHORS

Duchess Harris, JD, PhD

Dr. Harris is a professor of American Studies at Macalester College and curator of the Duchess Harris Collection of ABDO books. She is also the coauthor of the titles in the collection, which features popular selections such as *Hidden Human Computers: The Black Women of NASA* and series including News Literacy and Being Female in America.

Before working with ABDO, Dr. Harris authored several other books on the topics of race, culture, and American history. She served as an associate editor for *Litigation News*, the American Bar Association Section of Litigation's quarterly flagship publication, and was the first editor in chief of *Law Raza*, an interactive online journal covering race and the law, published at William Mitchell College of Law. She has earned a PhD in American Studies from the University of Minnesota and a JD from William Mitchell College of Law.

A. R. Carser

A. R. Carser is a freelance writer who lives in Minnesota. She enjoys learning and writing about history, culture, and society.

INDEX